D-DAY

Publisher's Note:

WIDE EYED EDITIONS

The Second World War, which lasted from 1939 to 1945, was the largest conflict the world has ever seen. It is remembered for the destructive power of its battles, the use of cutting-edge technology (including the first use of atomic weapons) and for the large-scale involvement of civilians. The war touched the lives of millions of people; for some this was because they joined the armed forces to fight, for others it was because they performed some other work that was necessary for the war effort. But even civilians who played no active role in the conflict were nonetheless affected by it. Millions of people had to move from their homes, either to escape the violence or because they had been forced to do so for political reasons. For some people this was a temporary move, for others it was permanent. An estimated 50-85 million people were killed in the war, most of whom were ordinary civilians.

The invasion relied on the hard work and dedication of many ordinary people. This book portrays D-Day through their eyes. It follows the story of the invasion, from the planning to the landings, to the aftermath, through their experiences and memories. There are stories of soldiers, from both Allied and Axis sides. Ordinary people for the most part, who took up arms simply because their countries asked them to and who did their very best because it was what seemed right at the time.

This book also follows non-combat personnel, including planners and medics, sailors and commanders. Then there were the civilians – people who were involved in D-Day because they sought it out, such as journalists intent on telling the world what was happening. Then there were those whom the war sought out, people whose ordinary lives were interrupted by the arrival of troops in strange uniforms and speaking foreign languages.

These are stories of bravery, sacrifice and innovation.

The World, June 1944

Arctic
Ocean

U.S.A.

Canada

U.S.A.

Atlantic
Ocean

Pacific
Ocean

Brazil

Bolivia

Norway

Finland

USSR

United
Kingdom

Netherlands

Belgium

Germany

Poland

Czechoslovakia

Hungary

France

Italy

Romania

Bulgaria

Yugoslavia

Greece

South
Africa

Southern
Ocean

The war started after a political party known as the Nazis took control of Germany. The Nazis were cruel and sought to harm many people, especially minority groups. Six million Jewish men, women, and children across Europe were rounded-up and murdered or worked to death in concentration camps because of their beliefs and heritage. Groups including Roma, people with disabilities, LGBT people, and others met a similar fate.

They also had plans to expand Germany's borders and to make it the most powerful country in Europe by invading other European countries. They treated people in the invaded countries with great cruelty, using their resources, including people, to make Germany stronger.

In September 1939 Nazi Germany invaded Poland, which led Britain and France to declare war on Germany. Despite this, Germany continued to invade other countries including France in 1940 and, in 1941, the Soviet Union, a vast union of countries in eastern Europe and Asia, dominated by Russia.

In December of that year Japan, which was friendly with Germany, attacked the United States. This prompted war between those two countries and fighting around the Pacific Ocean. Soon after this, Germany declared war on the United States, ensuring that the conflict would take place between two groups: **the Axis Powers, led by Germany, Italy and Japan, and the Allies, led by Britain, the Soviet Union and the United States.** Other countries, including Canada, South Africa, India, Australia and New Zealand, were drawn in to the fighting because they were part of European empires and held allegiance to countries such as Britain.

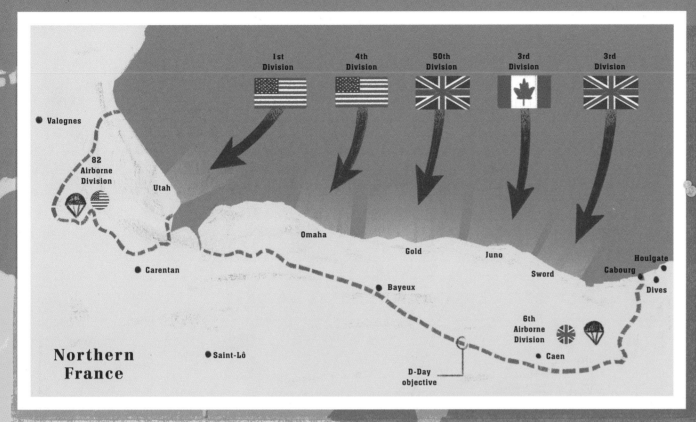

1st Division · 4th Division · 50th Division · 3rd Division · 3rd Division

Northern France

Valognes

82 Airborne Division

Utah

Carentan

Omaha

Gold

Juno

Sword

Houlgate

Cabourg

Dives

Bayeux

Saint-Lô

D-Day objective

6th Airborne Division

Caen

China

Japan

India

Pacific Ocean

Indian Ocean

Australia

New Zealand

● Allied forces

● Axis forces

● Nazi occupied countries

▥ Italy: Site of Allied southern campaign, still partially occupied by Nazi forces

Intense fighting took place between Germany and the Soviet Union in what was known as the 'Eastern Front'. The Soviet Union was keen for Britain, the US and their allies to attack from the west. An agreement was made that the Allies would invade western Europe and force Germany to fight on two fronts at once – the Eastern, against the Soviet Union, and the Western, against the remaining Allies.

At the same time, Allied forces attacked from the south through Italy, which was Germany's ally. **The most destructive fighting in European history occurred when all three fronts, Eastern, Western and Italian became active.** This book tells the story of the opening of the Western Front, an event that is known as the Normandy Invasion, the Normandy Landings, or simply D-Day. The invasion was made on five beaches in northern France, **with the aim of landing Allied troops on the continent so that they could push the German army out of France, Belgium and the Netherlands before continuing into Germany itself.**

The invasion was a colossal undertaking. It took months of intensive planning, much of it in complete secrecy, and close collaboration between the countries. Thousands of soldiers and sailors took part in the invasion itself and they were supported by many hundreds of other military staff and civilians, each one of whom contributed a small part to this giant collective effort. It was a dangerous and risky endeavour and success was far from certain. **At stake was the future of Europe, indeed the world itself, and the people involved in planning the invasion took their work very seriously.**

The war carried on for another year after D-Day. Fighting continued and the Allies pressed steadily on from east and west until they reached the German capital, Berlin, and prompted the Nazis to surrender. The war continued in the Pacific for a few more months until it too stopped in August 1945 with the surrender of Japan. The Allies won the Second World War through hard effort and sacrifice. Although D-Day was a major turning point in the conflict, it was just one part of a huge historical event. **The men and women who made D-Day happen each played their own small part too.**

This is their story.

Helen Denton

Taking part in this war has brought me from my home in South Dakota, USA, to stay for a while in London, England.

I work for General Dwight Eisenhower, who is the Supreme Commander of the Allied Forces in Europe and is a very important and busy man. Everything I do has to be kept top secret. I'm not even allowed to tell my family what I do, other than to say that I'm a Corporal in the Women's Army Corps.

Typing out General Eisenhower's lists of ships, details of places, amounts of supplies and soldiers, it has become obvious what we are doing – we, that is the Americans, the British, the Canadians and quite a few other countries, are going to invade Europe!

The Allies have been determined to attack the Axis Powers for some time now. The plan is to send the soldiers first to France, where they will set up a base, and from there move westwards into Europe, fighting the enemy until they reach Berlin, the capital city of Germany. The overall mission is codenamed Operation Overlord, while the invasion itself is called Operation Neptune. Most people call it D-Day, which simply means *Day Day*, that is, the day on which it will all happen.

Over a thousand planes will be used to carry bombs and paratroopers. There are even more ships and boats, over 5,000 in total. All in all, we will send 160,000 soldiers and sailors to France in just one day. More will follow and there will be over two million there by the end of the summer.

Together with British General Bernard Montgomery, General Eisenhower decided that Normandy in Northern France is the best place to start the invasion. They have selected five beaches on which to make the landings. Each beach has a codename. Two of them, Utah and Omaha, will be attacked by Americans, while the remaining three, Gold, Juno and Sword, will be attacked by British and Canadian forces.

The landings will be very difficult. Although we have chosen Normandy because it is less well defended than other parts of France, it is still dangerous. The Germans have set up machine guns to shoot at soldiers attempting to land, and have put large concrete and steel objects in the way, so that moving up the beach will be difficult.

We don't know when the landings will happen. It all depends on the weather as, if it is too wet and windy, crossing the sea will be difficult. General Eisenhower has a special team who are looking at the weather so that they can advise the best time to launch.

The landings will be made by air and sea. First, planes will bomb the area. Then, paratroopers will be taken over by planes during the night to secure the beaches ready for the main force in the daytime. They won't be able to make it completely safe... the Germans know that we will be planning something and have sent lots of their soldiers to the French coast to defend it.

Additional information

• Once the Allies had made it into France, General Eisenhower took his headquarters there too. Helen travelled across the Channel in the middle of the night and landed on Omaha Beach, from where she was taken to her new workplace in France.

• Although a lot of work was done in the few months before the landings, an invasion had been planned for years. After Germany attacked the Soviet Union (Russia) in 1941, the Russians were keen for the Allies to attack Germany from the west. There was a lot of pressure on the world leaders to do so.

• Preparation for the invasion meant that thousands of American and Canadian troops and other personnel came to southern England to train.

• Staff at headquarters used the latest technology to communicate and process information. The photo on the opposite page shows members of the US Women's Army Corps using teletype machines to send written messages over the airwaves.

Lieutenant General
Frederick Morgan

I joined the army in 1913, just before the outbreak of the First World War and fought as a junior officer.

In this Second World War, I am a senior commander. My official title is Chief of Staff to the Supreme Allied Commander or COSSAC. I work with almost a thousand people and our main task is to plan the invasion of Europe. The attack is getting closer every day and my unit has been absorbed into Supreme Headquarters Allied Expeditionary Force, which we call SHAEF for short (it rhymes with 'safe'). It is the top unit of command for the Allies in Europe.

We set up this unit so that all the senior commanders from the USA and the UK could work together. The overall commander, General Dwight D. Eisenhower, is American but his Deputy, Air Chief Marshal Arthur Tedder, is British. We tend to find that dividing responsibility between the Americans and the British works very well under the circumstances.

My role is to look at possible locations for our invasion and to assess each one for suitability. Our men will be vulnerable to attack and poor weather during the crossing and some of our boats and planes will need to travel there and back several times. The shortest possible route, which runs from Dover in England to Calais in France, might seem like a good idea. However, the Germans are expecting that and have defended the area heavily.

American born Major General Walter Bedell Smith is my immediate boss. He can get angry at times, but we get on very well and make a good team. We work in London but are planning to take our operation to France once our soldiers successfully invade the country.

Some of the options make particularly good landing spots because of their terrain, cliffs, rivers and canals. But it's not just about the landing – our soldiers need to push towards Germany once they land. Our chosen site will need access to road systems and as few obstacles as possible. We know that the Germans have defended the coast all the way up to Norway, but a northerly invasion would make onward travel difficult. It has to be France.

United Kingdom

Dover

Calais

Southhampton

Normandy

France

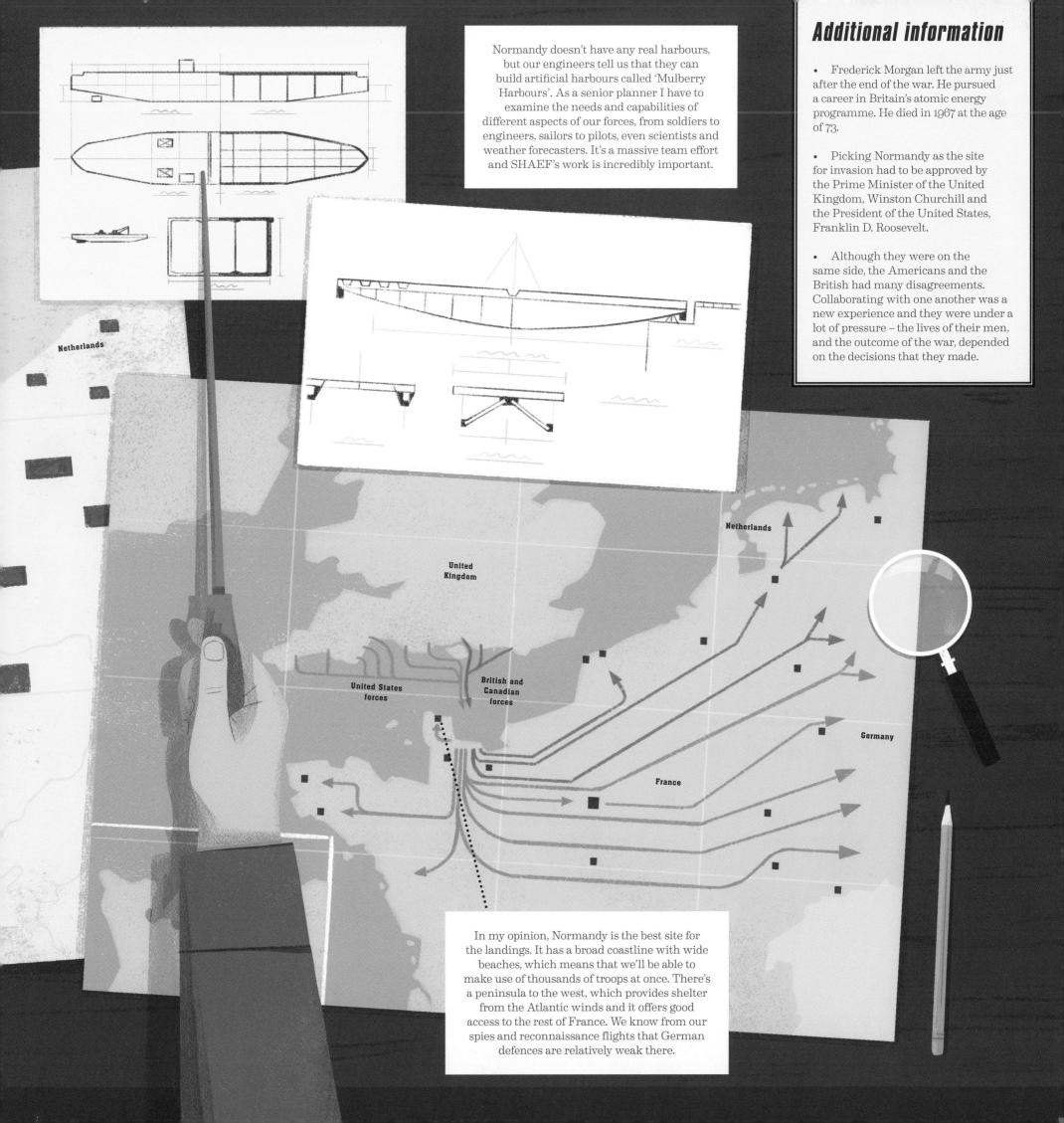

Normandy doesn't have any real harbours, but our engineers tell us that they can build artificial harbours called 'Mulberry Harbours'. As a senior planner I have to examine the needs and capabilities of different aspects of our forces, from soldiers to engineers, sailors to pilots, even scientists and weather forecasters. It's a massive team effort and SHAEF's work is incredibly important.

Netherlands

United Kingdom

United States forces

British and Canadian forces

Netherlands

Germany

France

In my opinion, Normandy is the best site for the landings. It has a broad coastline with wide beaches, which means that we'll be able to make use of thousands of troops at once. There's a peninsula to the west, which provides shelter from the Atlantic winds and it offers good access to the rest of France. We know from our spies and reconnaissance flights that German defences are relatively weak there.

General Field Marshal
Erwin Rommel

The German nation felt humiliated during the 1920s. Our enemies claimed victory in the First World War and punished us by fining us and taking some of our territory. Since the 1930s, we have been trying to take some of this territory back.

We now dominate Europe, but that leaves us with a lot of territory to defend. We know that the British and Americans are going to attack. We've been at war with them for years and, while there has been heavy fighting at sea, in the air, in North Africa and Italy, the western fringes of Europe have largely been left alone. There have been attempts of course, but we Germans successfully pushed back.

But they are now planning something big. We, the Germans, have been fighting the Soviet Union in Russia since 1941. The Soviets are on the same side as the British and Americans and they are desperate for them to attack us from the west, meaning we would be surrounded. If they succeed in invading the continent, we'll be defeated.

My task is to supervise the 'Atlantic Wall'. This is a series of defences we have built along the western edges of the continent, from south west France to the northern coasts of Norway. It's a colossal project but the enemy can attack us anywhere along that coastline.

The mines are the deadliest of all. These are bombs that sit just below the surface of the water or are buried in shallow ground. If something touches one of these, they explode. They're horrible, treacherous weapons to use but we have to take every possible precaution. This is going to be a very hard battle.

The enemy won't find it easy to land. We've placed steel units on the beaches to prevent their tanks from moving up the sand. They're just angled bits of metal, but are very effective. We call them hedgehogs. Rows of long spikes add more difficulties for the invading forces. They look like something from the Middle Ages, but they work well.

Additional information

• Erwin Rommel did not survive the war. Although he was considered a hero in Germany, and even won the respect of his opponents for his skill as a military commander, he became involved in a plot to kill the Nazi leader Adolf Hitler. Still, he was given a hero's funeral.

• Surrounding the Germans in Europe was the primary goal of the Normandy invasion. The Allied commanders knew that Germany was fighting hard against the Soviets in eastern Europe and that if they were forced to fight in the west at the same time, they would almost certainly be defeated. German commanders such as Rommel were desperate to prevent the Allies from landing in Western Europe as they knew that it would spell the end for them.

• The German leadership of this time could be cruel and harsh. When they took over a different country, they would use its resources, including people, to achieve their military aims. Many of the Atlantic Wall defences were built by non-Germans who were forced to work for free or face violence.

We have spies working to find out where the enemy will attack. Ideally, we'd know exactly where to place our strongest defences but that's not possible. We can guess where the enemy will attack us. Calais seems obvious, as it is closest to Great Britain. We've placed a lot of defences there but I'm sure the attackers will have counted on that.

Our engineers have designed strong walls and defences, including gun emplacements, barriers and observation points. They've been built by the people we captured, which makes it easier for us, but it's still going to be difficult.

■ = Atlantic wall

Norway

United Kingdom

German Empire

Calais

France

We're looking for as little cloud as possible, no rain, and light winds. Our men need good light so that they can see what they're doing. Our ships and aircraft work better when there's little wind and we expect that once the fighting starts there'll be a lot of smoke. If it's too windy, there'll be chaos on the battlefield.

5 JUNE, 1944

6 JUNE, 1944

Lawrence Hogben

Now that we know the target is Normandy, General Eisenhower says that he wants a full moon, a low tide and good weather.

We can predict the moon and the tides with 100% accuracy – we'll have them on the 5th, 6th and 7th June. But the weather? That's a bit more difficult.

I'm originally from New Zealand and I'm a Lieutenant in the Royal Navy. I'm a meteorologist, and I work as part of a team of six. We operate in twos, each pair communicating with the others by telephone. When I say 'communicating', I really mean 'arguing'. We rarely agree on anything, which just goes to show how difficult it is to predict the weather.

Additional information

• Hogben left the Royal Navy after the war and began a long career in industry. In later life, he enjoyed a retirement in France where he died in 2005, aged 98.

• The invasion was launched on Tuesday 6th June 1944. The weather was not perfect but the conditions were better than they had been on the 5th June.

• People didn't have access to sophisticated computers and satellites at the time. The uncertainty of predicting the weather, along with the very high stakes, placed the meteorologists under a lot of pressure, which is one reason why they had so many arguments.

The weather for the 5th looks bad. Overcast sky, low cloud cover and winds that are slightly stronger than we'd like. It's the wrong day for it. We should delay. But it's not our decision to make – all we can do is to make our case to the High Command and leave it to them. It helps that all six of us finally agree.

We take measurements and data from our weather stations around the coast, from ships at sea and from balloons in the air. We even take data from the enemy; our codebreakers have managed to crack their radio code and we've been listening in to their communications for months. We use all of this information to track weather patterns as they shift and move about. The goal is to work out what weather pattern will be over the target area at the right time.

We can't delay forever and with the moon and the tides being where they are, it will have to be this week. Will the 6th be better than the 5th? One way or another, it's going to be a gamble. I'm glad that the final decision is not mine to make, but if we go for the 6th, it will be because of the weather forecast more than anything else. That's quite something for a meteorologist like me to consider.

On the night of the attack, our plan is to fly in five large formations made of over 100 planes and several ships and boats below. My own aerial unit is made up of 16 Lancaster bombers. This will make it look like there is a large convoy heading towards Cap d'Antifer, which is nearly 100 miles away from where the real invasion is going to land.

Dave Shannon

I'm an Australian pilot in the RAAF (Royal Australian Air Force) but I've spent the past couple of years in Great Britain, flying planes for the RAF.

I drop thousands of pieces of metal and plastic out of my plane. We call the pieces 'window' while our American friends call it 'chaff'. It looks like silver confetti but it's actually the latest technology. If you scatter enough it can confuse radar.

Radar works by sending out little radio waves, like sounds, and detecting where those sounds bounce off objects. This helps to form a picture of where things are. A cloud of 'window' strips will make it look like there is a large object in the sea and the Germans will think it is an invasion.

My job is to fly far away from where the real invasion is taking place and make it look as though the attacking force is here. We're supported by boats that travel out in the English Channel and float huge balloons above them. These also appear on radar and confuse the enemy.

The Germans won't know where the real invasion is and will have to send their soldiers and planes to lots of places at once, meaning there will be fewer people to defend the invasion site. This should make it easier for our men to break through once they attack.

We've been training for this mission for several weeks. If we make a mistake, the Germans will know we're trying to fool them and that could be disastrous for the men leading the main attack. We have to work in close partnership with the boats beneath us, making it look as though we are moving as a single convoy.

We have to give the impression that we're all moving at seven knots and covering around 24 nautical miles over the course of the night. This is a good speed for a boat but very, very slow for an aircraft. We solve the problem by flying in circles, moving slightly ahead each time, and taking great care about when and where we drop the clouds of 'window'. It is extremely precise work and very tiring to perform.

Looking back now, I'm pleased to say that our mission was a success. Our comrades in England were able to test our performance by scanning the area with their own radar. Our patrol did indeed resemble a large convoy of ships, travelling steadily across the Channel. Further reports showed that the enemy set searchlights across the area and launched boats in pursuit of the fake 'invasion force'. Our deception was a success.

Additional information

• Dave received several medals for his service as a pilot. After the war he worked in the oil industry until his retirement. He died in 1993 at the age of 70.

• Radar (**RA**dio **D**etection **A**nd **R**anging) was developed over a long period of time. The use of radar was essential during the Second World War. It is still a key component of military technology today.

• Efforts to confuse radar are known as countermeasures and include creating a fake image or 'jamming' the enemy's radar by preventing it from developing a clear picture.

• In 1942 British troops parachuted into France near a German radar installation and stole the equipment. Analysis of these items allowed the Allies to make effective countermeasures against them and led indirectly to Dave Shannon's mission in 1944.

The Allies had to take control of the routes away from the beaches before they made their landings. The first soldiers to take part in the action were transported by air in the early hours of the morning and given the task of fighting off the German soldiers that were guarding these routes. This was a dangerous mission, and let the Germans know that the invasion was coming, but it was important work. Without doing this, the invasion would fail.

18-year-old Helmut was taught that it was important for Germany to become strong again. Before young soldiers like Helmut were even born, Germany had lost the First World War, and had been paying reparations with money and land ever since. This humiliation caused many German soldiers to believe they were simply taking back what they were owed.

Helmut Roemer

I was a typically boring guard duty the other night, looking after a canal bridge.

I have to stop anyone attempting to cross and check they have permission. Just after midnight, I heard a strange swishing noise and then thud! Several large gliders landed and some heavily armed soldiers jumped out. I let off a flare and ran away to hide. The soldiers were shouting in English. I thought they must have been the enemy – British, or possibly American. A fierce gunfight broke out but the enemy had the advantage and quickly took control of the bridge.

I hid for a long while, but, scared and ashamed, I finally decided to hand myself in. The British soldiers told me and the other captured Germans that we were their prisoners. Waiting on the beach for a boat to take us to England, I saw thousands and thousands of soldiers, hundreds of boats and lots of tanks and jeeps working to secure the area.

I asked one of the other prisoners if this was the army that was going to attack Germany. He laughed and said that it was only a small part of it...

The gliders were made from wood and were towed by powered aeroplanes. Once the aircraft were close to the landing site, the aeroplanes released the gliders which were piloted to the ground silently. This added to the sense of surprise and meant that the powered aircraft could be used again later on.

Helmut Roemer, along with countless other captured soldiers, remained a prisoner for the rest of the war. He was transported from cell to cell and stayed in prison camps in Britain and Canada. Although he feared being labelled a coward, prison life wasn't too bad and he was able to learn English.

Additional information

• The German armed forces, of which Helmut Roemer was a part, was called the Wehrmacht and comprised the German army, navy and air force. It was active for ten years (1935-1945), during which time over 18 million men served in its forces. Some volunteered but most were forced to join under a system called 'conscription'.

• Conscription also applied to British armed forces, which all men aged between 18 and 41 had to join unless they could give a good reason not to do so. In the USA, men were required to register with the government which then selected names to join the armed forces in a process known as the 'draft'.

• German soldiers were required to fight in both the Eastern and Western Fronts and were under a lot of pressure as the war went on. Many of their soldiers were young, ordinary men like in the photo on the opposite page, who were forced to fight.

Additional information

- Moreen survived the war and lived a long life, working as a guide in Portsmouth.

- Her brother's ship was attacked by the enemy. When this happened Moreen had no choice but to finish her shift but was relieved to find out later that her brother had survived.

- Plotters were in action throughout the war and were involved in many of the most important battles and events.

- Like Moreen, most of the plotters were young women. The authorities did not allow women to go out to the battlefields or pilot ships and aircraft, so plotting was a job that was seen as 'women's work'.

- There are far more photos of men from the war than there are of women. Countless women have been forgotten or haven't received the recognition they deserve because of this.

I work *underneath* a building in Portsmouth. Our room is in a bunker 30 metres underground. We sometimes joke that we're the safest people in England but it's for a good reason. We have to continue our work even if the enemy starts bombing Portsmouth, like they did four years ago.

It's very intense work and highly pressured. We have to be accurate and quick at the same time. It's important that the commanders have a real picture of what is going on at any given time. Making a mistake could have terrible consequences for our side. The lives of our crews, perhaps even victory in the war itself, all depend on what we do in this cramped, hot room.

Moreen James

In this job I feel as though I'm part of something much bigger than myself. Of course, it helps that my job is all about looking at the bigger picture.

I'm in the Women's Royal Naval Service (WRNS) but everyone calls us 'Wrens', like the bird. Which is appropriate, because I get a bird's eye view of the war. This image shows some of my colleagues hard at work.

I work as a plotter, keeping track of the movement of ships. There's so much traffic moving back and forth across the Channel that without a method for keeping track of everything, things would fall into confusion. It's important that the commanders always know where their boats and planes are. It would be impossible for them to control the situation unless they did.

A large map painted onto a table fills the room. It shows the coasts of Britain and France and the Channel in between. We place little figurines on the map which represent ships and move them around so their position on the map matches where they really are at the moment. By looking at the map, the commanders can see instantly where everybody is and get a picture of the situation as it happens in real time.

Everyone was expecting that the invasion would begin yesterday, but it was not to be. I think that the weather was too poor or something. But today is the day. Not only were the skies above Portsmouth full of aircraft heading south this morning, but when I started my shift, the invasion had already started.

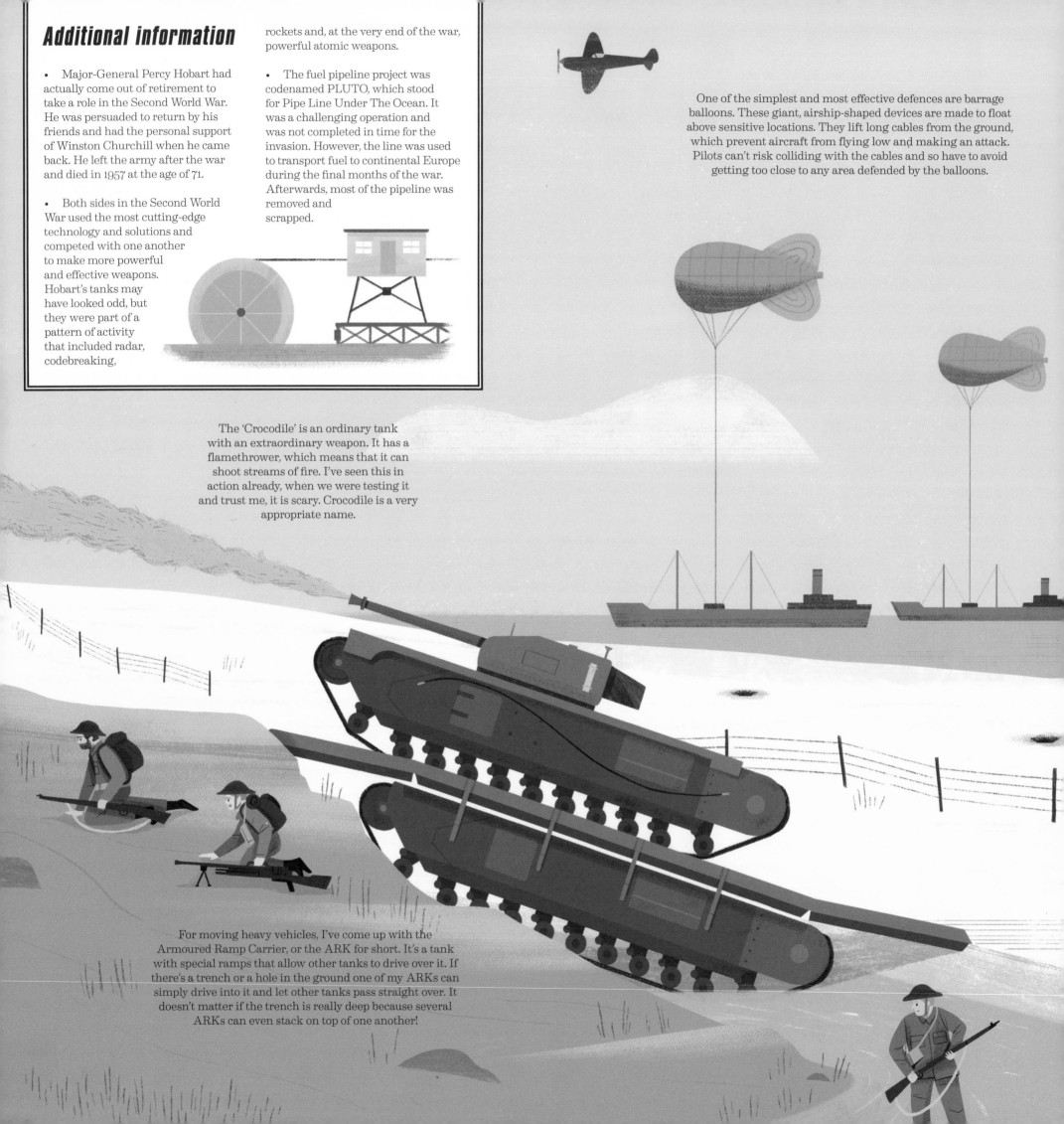

Additional information

• Major-General Percy Hobart had actually come out of retirement to take a role in the Second World War. He was persuaded to return by his friends and had the personal support of Winston Churchill when he came back. He left the army after the war and died in 1957 at the age of 71.

• Both sides in the Second World War used the most cutting-edge technology and solutions and competed with one another to make more powerful and effective weapons. Hobart's tanks may have looked odd, but they were part of a pattern of activity that included radar, codebreaking,

rockets and, at the very end of the war, powerful atomic weapons.

• The fuel pipeline project was codenamed PLUTO, which stood for Pipe Line Under The Ocean. It was a challenging operation and was not completed in time for the invasion. However, the line was used to transport fuel to continental Europe during the final months of the war. Afterwards, most of the pipeline was removed and scrapped.

One of the simplest and most effective defences are barrage balloons. These giant, airship-shaped devices are made to float above sensitive locations. They lift long cables from the ground, which prevent aircraft from flying low and making an attack. Pilots can't risk colliding with the cables and so have to avoid getting too close to any area defended by the balloons.

The 'Crocodile' is an ordinary tank with an extraordinary weapon. It has a flamethrower, which means that it can shoot streams of fire. I've seen this in action already, when we were testing it and trust me, it is scary. Crocodile is a very appropriate name.

For moving heavy vehicles, I've come up with the Armoured Ramp Carrier, or the ARK for short. It's a tank with special ramps that allow other tanks to drive over it. If there's a trench or a hole in the ground one of my ARKs can simply drive into it and let other tanks pass straight over. It doesn't matter if the trench is really deep because several ARKs can even stack on top of one another!

Major-General
Percy Hobart

I'm a soldier but my work is closer to that of an engineer than a fighter – you might even call me an inventor.

I specialise in tanks and in my view, tanks and other armoured vehicles are the future of warfare.

Take this current mission, the invasion of Normandy. It's going to be very difficult to get our men where they need to be. We're expecting a lot of resistance from the enemy, who will be armed with machine guns and other powerful weapons. The ground will be very difficult to get across – there's a lot of sand, some wet, some soft, as well as dunes, uneven terrain and even canals and rivers to get across.

It's my job to come up with the equipment the men will need. Most of my inventions are converted tanks which I make adaptations to so that they can do different jobs. My process is a simple one, I start with a problem that the soldiers are likely to face and then I look for a way of solving it.

Keeping our soldiers well-supplied is key to success. One of the things they will need is fuel to keep their tanks and jeeps going. Transporting this in barrels is too difficult and dangerous so our engineers have built an entire pipeline that will run under the sea and carry oil from France to England. It's an astonishing achievement and a mark of just how we are using ingenuity to fight this war.

One of the main problems in the invasion of Normandy is getting across the sand. It can be difficult enough walking across sand in normal footwear but imagine trying to do so while wearing battledress and carrying heavy equipment and with thousands of men in the same place, the ground is going to get churned up pretty quickly...

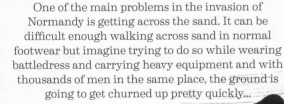

...but my invention, the 'bobbin', will help solve this problem. It is a tank with a special attachment that feeds out an artificial path for the soldiers to walk on.

Richard Winters

My name is Lieutenant Richard Winters, I'm American, born and raised in Pennsylvania. I'm 26 years old, which makes me ancient compared to some of my men!

We're paratroopers, trained to jump from planes so that we can reach the combat zone quickly. Most of the allies will be making the invasion by boat during the day. But not us – we came by air and at night. We were the first men on the ground, the first to face the danger and, hopefully, the first to make a success. Months of training and preparation have all led up to this very moment. My first thoughts are of my men. I'm responsible for them and they all rely on me...

We're called paratroopers because we use parachutes but that's only a tiny part of what we do. For the most part we're ordinary soldiers moving around on foot. As soon as we land we have to secure the area, prevent the Germans from controlling the territory and make it safe for the main invasion that will come later. Having airborne troops is a serious advantage. Troops like mine are a major factor of planning – if the invasion succeeds, it will largely be down to the things that my men and I do today, before the sun even comes up on D-Day.

Our immediate objective is to destroy the gun emplacements the Germans built. We know they've been preparing for our invasion and that they've put up armed defences all along the French coast. Each one of these emplacements can kill hundreds of our men as they arrive on the beaches. The more we destroy, the easier things will be for our comrades. Once the invasion has been made, we'll carry on fighting and we won't stop until we've beaten the enemy. It might take months, or even years…

The Germans were waiting for us as soon as our planes passed into French territory. The Anti-Aircraft Artillery (AAA) lit up the sky as their giant guns fired from the ground. I lost my weapon during the jump and First Lieutenant Meehan, the man in charge of our unit, was nowhere to be found once we landed. I can only assume that the guns got him, but I don't have time to dwell on that. With Meehan gone, I'm in charge of the unit.

Stanley Hollis VC

Everyone knows me as Stanley Hollis but now I get to call myself Stanley Hollis VC.

Those two little letters mean a lot. The 'VC' stands for 'Victoria Cross' and it's a medal – the highest honour that Britain awards to soldiers. The medal is awarded 'for valour', which is another way of saying 'bravery'.

I got my medal for my actions on D-Day. I've been told that I was the only person who has been awarded the VC for that day. Which is remarkable, given how brave everyone was on that eventful day.

When we spotted the first one I quickly rushed towards it before the enemy had a chance to aim at me. I took aim and shot as best I could through the peep-holes. Next, I jumped right on top of the pillbox and threw a grenade inside. A loud explosion told us we'd succeeded in destroying the pillbox. Two of the Germans had been killed while the rest we took as prisoners.

One of the conditions of being given the VC is that your act of bravery has to be done while 'in the presence of the enemy'. No one can argue about that – the enemy was certainly present where I was.

My unit and I were moving up the beach, looking for enemy positions. We had been given orders to investigate two of their 'pillboxes', which is what we call their gun emplacements. These structures are like bunkers, where the Germans hide and shoot at us. They can be hard to access because they're made of concrete and some are half-buried in the ground, which means we have to get really close to destroy them. Very dangerous stuff.

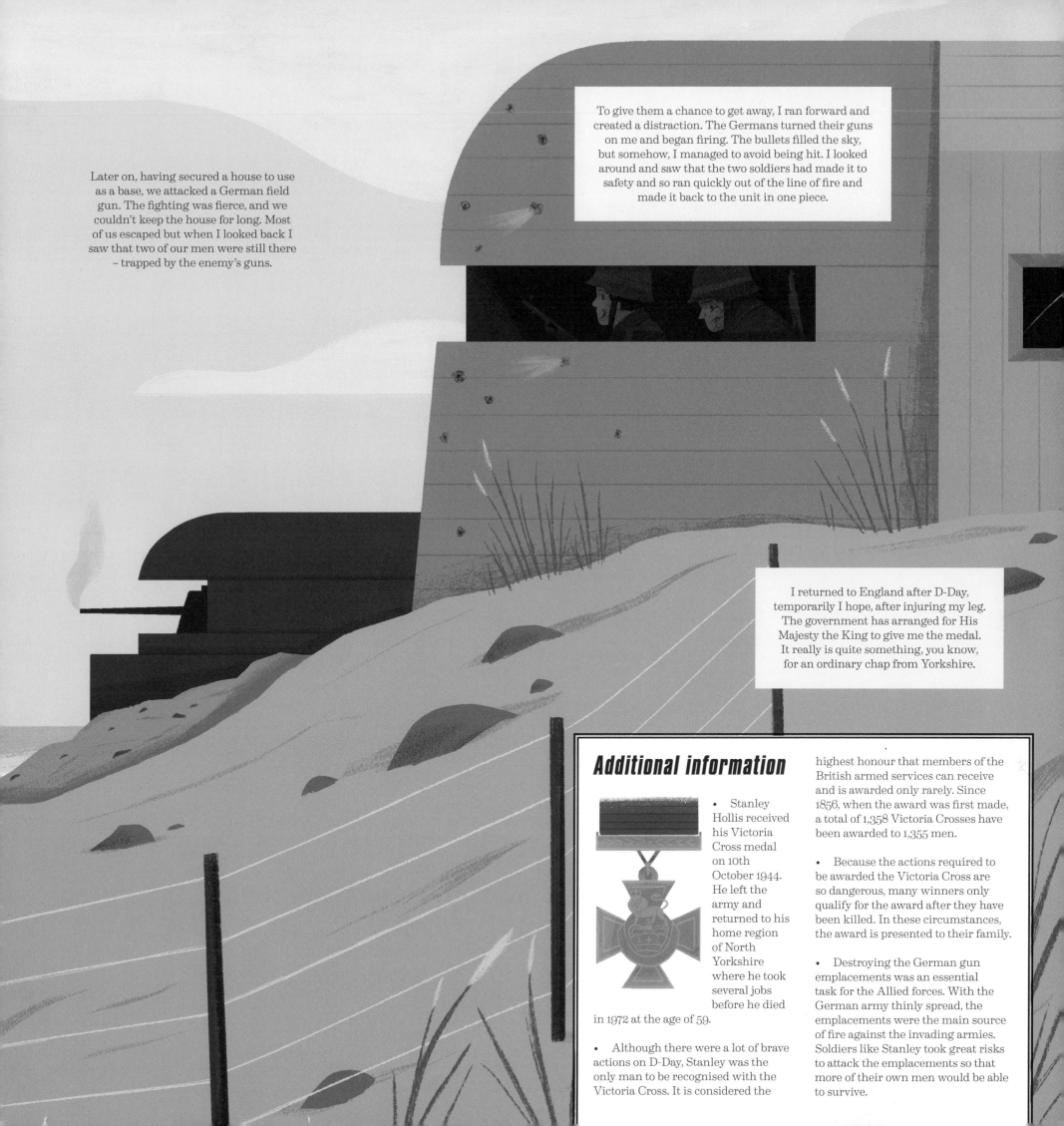

Later on, having secured a house to use as a base, we attacked a German field gun. The fighting was fierce, and we couldn't keep the house for long. Most of us escaped but when I looked back I saw that two of our men were still there – trapped by the enemy's guns.

To give them a chance to get away, I ran forward and created a distraction. The Germans turned their guns on me and began firing. The bullets filled the sky, but somehow, I managed to avoid being hit. I looked around and saw that the two soldiers had made it to safety and so ran quickly out of the line of fire and made it back to the unit in one piece.

I returned to England after D-Day, temporarily I hope, after injuring my leg. The government has arranged for His Majesty the King to give me the medal. It really is quite something, you know, for an ordinary chap from Yorkshire.

Additional information

- Stanley Hollis received his Victoria Cross medal on 10th October 1944. He left the army and returned to his home region of North Yorkshire where he took several jobs before he died in 1972 at the age of 59.

- Although there were a lot of brave actions on D-Day, Stanley was the only man to be recognised with the Victoria Cross. It is considered the highest honour that members of the British armed services can receive and is awarded only rarely. Since 1856, when the award was first made, a total of 1,358 Victoria Crosses have been awarded to 1,355 men.

- Because the actions required to be awarded the Victoria Cross are so dangerous, many winners only qualify for the award after they have been killed. In these circumstances, the award is presented to their family.

- Destroying the German gun emplacements was an essential task for the Allied forces. With the German army thinly spread, the emplacements were the main source of fire against the invading armies. Soldiers like Stanley took great risks to attack the emplacements so that more of their own men would be able to survive.

Waverly Bernard Woodson Jr

Everyone calls me Woody. I was born in 1922 and before the war I was a second-year medical student in my home state of Pennsylvania.

Although I wanted to complete my studies, I was eager to take part in the war. I wanted to join an Anti-Aircraft Artillery (AAA) unit but I was discouraged because those units are all-white. However, I was able to secure a position as a medic. My unit, the 320th Barrage Balloon Battalion, is made up entirely of African-Americans like me.

I believe that I contributed far more with my first aid kit than I would have done with an artillery piece. Never was this truer than when I landed in Normandy. That was one very, very long day.

When we made it to the shore the scale of the task became horrifyingly clear. There were dying and injured men everywhere. Some of the injured were easy to deal with. They just needed bandaging up like me. I told them, 'I've been hit myself. If I can carry on, then so can you'. Many of them were able to get up and get on with their mission once I had attended to them. Others took more work.

We hit a mine on our way to the shore which violently rocked our vessel. The very next instant, a second explosion hit us. This one was a shell, fired from the shore. Small bits of metal called shrapnel fly out when a shell explodes, and when that shell exploded I felt a sharp pain in my leg and bottom. I was covered in blood. I had been hit by shrapnel. Another medic helped me apply bandages to stem the bleeding. But I couldn't quit. There was too much to do.

Additional information

• Waverly made a full recovery from his injuries. After the war he qualified as a doctor. He served in the Korean War (1950-53) and enjoyed a long career in the medical profession.

• During the Second World War, the United States Army operated separate units for white and black soldiers in a policy called 'segregation'. Black soldiers were treated with less respect than white ones and even a brave and dedicated soldier like Waverly could be overlooked for recognition.

• The job of a combat medic like Waverly is to stabilise the patient so that he can survive long enough to be taken to hospital. Their main aims are to ensure that the patient can breathe and that his wounds are bandaged. They also provide painkillers to help the injured soldier to cope.

• Most medics are unarmed. They have to carry medical equipment and other supplies, so holding a weapon would be difficult. They can be identified by the red cross painted on their uniform and many armies try not to aim at the other side's medics. It is still a very dangerous job and a combat medic can be killed or injured just as easily as a regular soldier.

I gave some of the men injections of morphine, which is a really powerful painkiller. If a man had lost a lot of blood, I gave him blood plasma, which meant that his body could continue working long enough for the team to get him to a hospital. I worked all day, through the night and into daylight again. Eventually, the work became too much, and I had to stop and rest. I was taken to a hospital ship offshore where my wounds were treated properly and where, finally, I could sleep and recover.

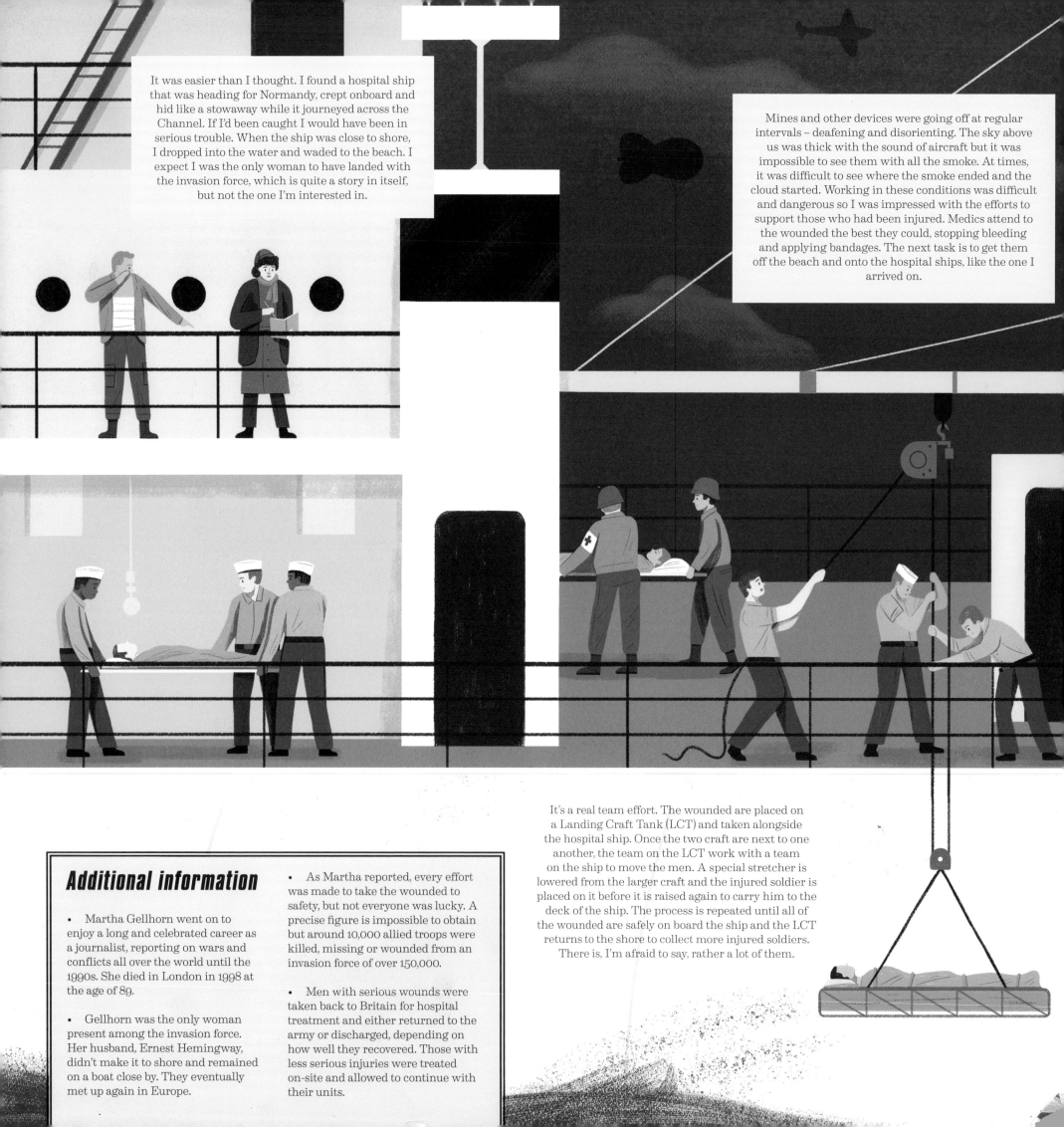

It was easier than I thought. I found a hospital ship that was heading for Normandy, crept onboard and hid like a stowaway while it journeyed across the Channel. If I'd been caught I would have been in serious trouble. When the ship was close to shore, I dropped into the water and waded to the beach. I expect I was the only woman to have landed with the invasion force, which is quite a story in itself, but not the one I'm interested in.

Mines and other devices were going off at regular intervals – deafening and disorienting. The sky above us was thick with the sound of aircraft but it was impossible to see them with all the smoke. At times, it was difficult to see where the smoke ended and the cloud started. Working in these conditions was difficult and dangerous so I was impressed with the efforts to support those who had been injured. Medics attend to the wounded the best they could, stopping bleeding and applying bandages. The next task is to get them off the beach and onto the hospital ships, like the one I arrived on.

It's a real team effort. The wounded are placed on a Landing Craft Tank (LCT) and taken alongside the hospital ship. Once the two craft are next to one another, the team on the LCT work with a team on the ship to move the men. A special stretcher is lowered from the larger craft and the injured soldier is placed on it before it is raised again to carry him to the deck of the ship. The process is repeated until all of the wounded are safely on board the ship and the LCT returns to the shore to collect more injured soldiers. There is, I'm afraid to say, rather a lot of them.

Additional information

• Martha Gellhorn went on to enjoy a long and celebrated career as a journalist, reporting on wars and conflicts all over the world until the 1990s. She died in London in 1998 at the age of 89.

• Gellhorn was the only woman present among the invasion force. Her husband, Ernest Hemingway, didn't make it to shore and remained on a boat close by. They eventually met up again in Europe.

• As Martha reported, every effort was made to take the wounded to safety, but not everyone was lucky. A precise figure is impossible to obtain but around 10,000 allied troops were killed, missing or wounded from an invasion force of over 150,000.

• Men with serious wounds were taken back to Britain for hospital treatment and either returned to the army or discharged, depending on how well they recovered. Those with less serious injuries were treated on-site and allowed to continue with their units.

Martha Gellhorn

I'm Martha Gellhorn and I'm a journalist. The Allied forces allow journalists to accompany soldiers on their mission so that they can report on what they're doing – it's a good way of finding out what's going on in the war.

For this invasion, each newspaper was allowed to send just one journalist. I was annoyed when the magazine I work for, *Collier's,* chose to send my husband, Ernest Hemingway, instead of me. He's more famous than I am but I'm a fine journalist and the job should have been mine. But I wasn't going to give up quite so easily and, determined not to miss out on the biggest story of the year, I decided to sneak my way in.

I wanted to report on the treatment of the wounded soldiers and the effect that the landings were having on local civilians. With everything that's going on, the size of the invasion and the astonishing use of technology and firepower, it would be all too easy to forget the ordinary men, women and children whose lives are affected by the fighting. As a journalist, I see it as my duty to bring their stories to wider attention.

Additional information

• General Field Marshal Gerd von Rundstedt stayed with the German army until they were defeated in 1945 and he was captured by the Americans. He was imprisoned in Britain where he suffered from declining health. Like many senior German officers, he was put on trial but was eventually released back to Germany. He died in 1953, aged 77.

• Although the German defenders put up a fierce fight against the invading forces, they were badly organised and relatively weak. Gerd von Rundstedt was one of the few senior commanders to recognise the scale of the threat to Germany and

to understand what kind of defence would need to be mounted. However, the disorganised and badly-led regime did not take his advice, which proved costly to the Germans.

• The energy that the Allies put into creating distractions and diversions worked very well indeed and the choice of Normandy for their assault came as a surprise to the Germans. The long and careful planning proved to be worth the effort.

• By the time of the invasion of Normandy, Germany was in a difficult position. Their war against the Soviet Union was going badly for them and they had to spend a lot of effort in the east. The attacks in France made the war impossible for them.

It would take us longer to send troops to the coast of France than to, say, the Netherlands. It seemed obvious to me that they would strike at Calais. It offers the shortest possible crossing from Britain to France, which is a considerable advantage. As we have so few soldiers available it made sense for us to place most of them there. I regret that now.

The enemy can choose exactly when and where they will make the invasion. They will want as many hours of daylight as possible, so June seems the likeliest month for it to happen. France seems like the most obvious choice to land because it's the closest country to Great Britain while being far enough away from Germany for them to organise their forces before pressing on.

Thousands and thousands of ships, boats and other small craft filled the area. The fighting was fierce on the beaches; we gave as good a response as we could, but we were soon overwhelmed. The enemy was well-fed and well-equipped while we, on the other hand, had poorly-supported and badly trained teenage conscripts. Many of them were not even German, they were Poles, Czechs and Ukrainians that we'd taken from the east and forced to fight in the west. They didn't care whether Germany was defeated and surrendered easily. They just wanted to survive. When the enemy began to arrive in such large numbers, survival was all we could really hope for.

In the early hours of the 6th June American paratroopers began to land. To my great shock, they didn't land in Calais, but in Normandy, which is 100 miles away. This could only mean that thousands more soldiers would be on their way from Britain to Normandy within a matter of hours. Our side was in total chaos. I had long argued that we needed a lot of tanks in France, ready for the invasion but I was ignored. Our position was getting worse with every minute of delay.

General Field Marshal
Gerd von Rundstedt

It's my job to lead the German defence against the invaders. Part of me thinks it should have been easier – after all, we are defending, rather than attacking.

We control most of the continent and we had, in theory, a lot of time to prepare. But the trouble is, so did the invaders. We knew they'd been planning this for years and that they put a lot of time, energy and money into preparations. We, on the other hand, have spent the past three years fighting a brutal and violent war against the Russians in the east. Most of our soldiers are over there and we can't afford to bring many of them here to France. I spent some time in the east myself; I know how bad it is there.

We perform in a complicated formation called the 'fluid six'. We fly in three pairs, in three rows of two. The aircraft on the left-hand side fly higher than the ones in the middle, which fly higher than the ones on the right. We have to maintain the same relative altitude to keep the formation, which is difficult but worth it. The fluid six means that we can provide cover for one another in case of attack by enemy aircraft.

My job as a Spitfire pilot is highly skilled and very dangerous. Piloting an aircraft is a demanding job and during combat it becomes even more difficult. I have to keep my mind on the mission, deal with enemy aircraft, stay alert to weapons fired from the ground and maintain a close formation with my colleagues. There's one of us in each aircraft but we are very much a team.

Additional information

• Michel Donnet completed his mission on D-Day and continued to fly missions with the RAF until the end of the war. He returned to Belgium after peace was declared and continued to enjoy a military career. He died in 2013 at the age of 96.

• Belgium was liberated by the Allies in September 1944. Michel led a formation of 12 Spitfires over the capital city Brussels in celebration.

• Many people from occupied countries fought as part of the Allied forces in the war. In addition to Belgians like Michel Donnet, there were French, Poles, Czechoslovakians, Norwegians and many more. Their skills and commitment were highly valued by the Allied commanders.

• The fighter aircraft used at D-Day were decorated with black-and-white 'invasion stripes'. The confusion of battle meant that it was possible for planes to be shot by people from the same side. The stripes were intended to make it easier for fighters to recognise their own side's aircraft.

• The most famous plane used by the Royal Air Force was the Supermarine Spitfire, like the one shown in this photo. It was a single-seat fighter plane that was used to attack enemy aircraft and protect ground troops.

Michel Donnet

My name is Michel Donnet, but everyone calls me Mike, especially in England, which is where I've been living since 1941.

I'm from Belgium where I was a pilot in the Air Force, but my country was taken over by the Germans and I was imprisoned. When I was released, I escaped to England where I joined the Royal Air Force. They were impressed that my fellow escapee and I had built our own plane to escape in! I'm not the only Belgian in the RAF, in fact, there's a whole squadron of us. We've done a lot for the war effort and have flown many dangerous missions. But today we're getting ready to go back home. It will take quite a while though because we're starting with France and the aim is to free all the countries that have been occupied by the Germans. I cannot wait until we get into Belgium.

Teamwork like this helps us to focus on our main mission, which for D-Day means providing air cover. The Germans will send their fighter aircraft as soon as they know the invasion is under way so it's our job to fly in and attack them. Our priority is to keep the ground safe for our troops. The air will be thick with smoke and heavy with bullets. Some of these will be aimed at us while others will be those from the battle below. We've trained hard for this mission, but this will be my most intense one yet.

My journey across the Channel was simple in theory. The plan was to drive the truck onto a special boat called a Landing Ship Transport (LST). We knew there wouldn't be a dedicated dock to disembark on when we reached France, so the LST towed a special raft called a 'rhino'. As the LST approached the shore, the rhino would move to the front, where it could act like a floating ramp. I would drive onto the rhino, which would float closer to shore until I could drive straight off onto the beach. Like I said, simple – in theory.

However, it was much different in practice. The water was rough and jerked the rhino around like it was a small toy. And as I made my transfer onto the rhino the LST jolted and hit the underside of my truck. I knew this would cause me trouble when I moved onto shore. Bullets were flying through the air as I tried to drive the truck forward. There was something wrong with it and I had no choice but to try to fix it there and then.

Additional information

- Willie Pound returned to Canada after the war and died in November 2016. In 2012 he was honoured with the Queen Elizabeth II Diamond Jubilee Medal for his role in D-Day.

- Over 14,000 Canadians took part in the D-Day landings, mainly on the beach codenamed 'Juno', which they assaulted in partnership with British troops. The Royal Canadian Navy also provided 110 ships and 10,000 sailors in support roles. On D-Day itself, 1074 Canadians became casualties with 359 of them killed.

- The effort to provide soldiers with supplies was as large and important as the military invasion itself. Men like Willie Pound helped to move over half a million tonnes of supplies. They needed nearly 200,000 vehicles to do so.

- Large trucks made good targets for enemy guns and their crews faced great danger in providing the supplies. There were few opportunities for sleep in the first days of the invasion and crews had to take what rest they could in their trucks. Some crews, like Willie's, slept underneath their trucks to find safety from the gunfire.

- Vehicles, from motorbikes to lorries. were very important in the Second World War and used to transport people, goods, weapons and supplies. The image at the bottom of this page is an RAF transport convoy in North Africa

But in all the confusion and panic I managed to get lost. I drove around and around trying to keep calm until eventually I saw a sign with a maple leaf on it – the symbol of Canada. It was such a relief to see our fellow countrymen. They were paratroopers who laughed when we told them where we'd been. It turned out that we'd been moving through enemy territory – what a lucky escape we'd had!

I got underneath the truck and found that the booster brake had been damaged – most likely by the jolting of the LST and rhino. I worked to get it unstuck while my colleagues in the truck yelled at me to get a move on. We were all panicking, but I had to concentrate. Finally, I managed to solve the problem, got back in the cab and drove the vehicle up onto the beach.

Willie Pound

I'm Willie Pound from Brighton, Ontario and I'm a Private in the Canadian Army.

I come from a military family; my two older brothers are also in the forces. I drive a three-tonne truck, which is the largest one used by the Canadian Army. It can carry a lot of gear, including soldiers when required. With so many men and so much equipment needed, trucks like mine are essential. Our work involves carrying food rations for the soldiers, so they are usually pleased to see us arrive!

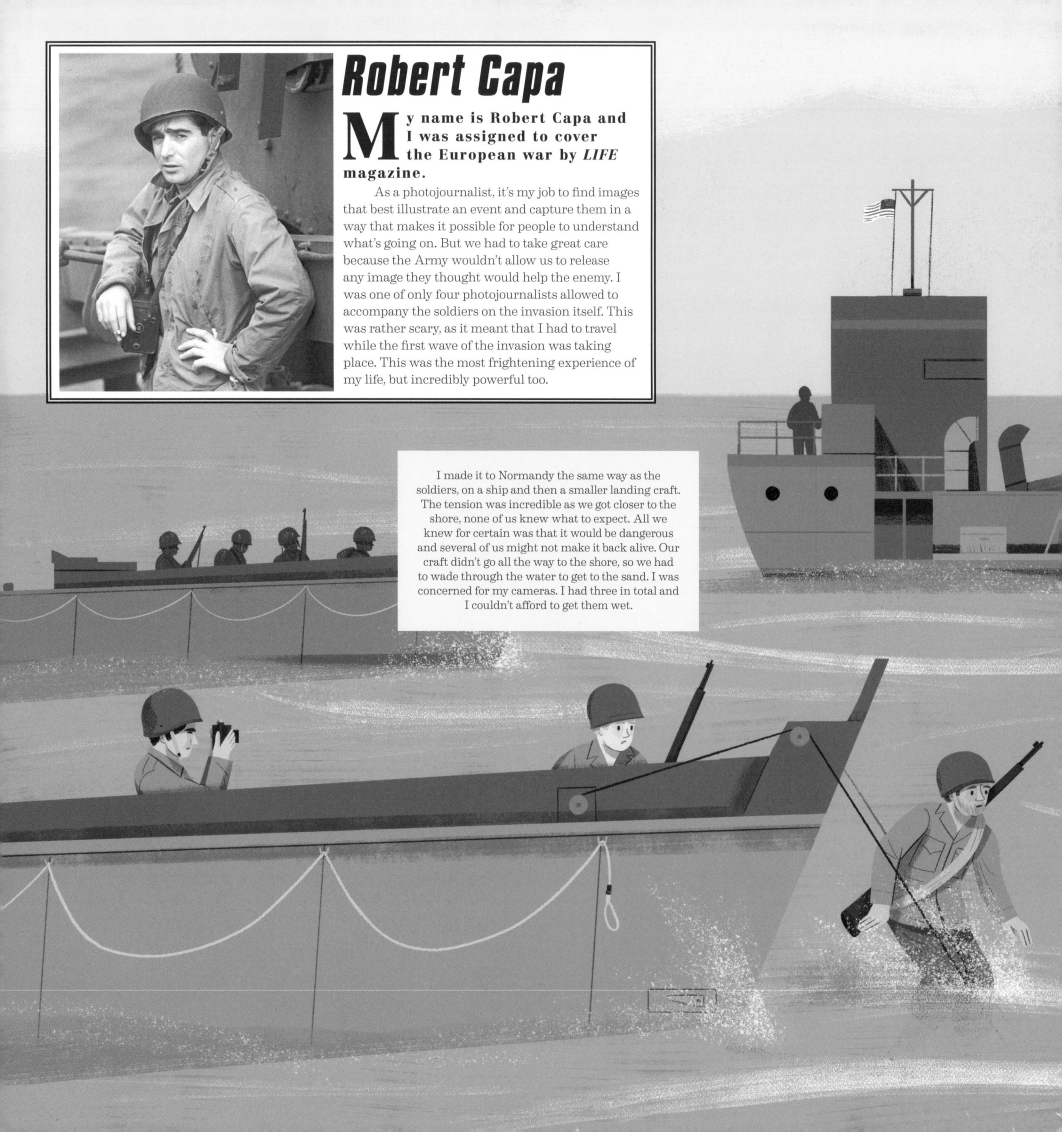

Robert Capa

My name is Robert Capa and I was assigned to cover the European war by *LIFE* magazine.

As a photojournalist, it's my job to find images that best illustrate an event and capture them in a way that makes it possible for people to understand what's going on. But we had to take great care because the Army wouldn't allow us to release any image they thought would help the enemy. I was one of only four photojournalists allowed to accompany the soldiers on the invasion itself. This was rather scary, as it meant that I had to travel while the first wave of the invasion was taking place. This was the most frightening experience of my life, but incredibly powerful too.

I made it to Normandy the same way as the soldiers, on a ship and then a smaller landing craft. The tension was incredible as we got closer to the shore, none of us knew what to expect. All we knew for certain was that it would be dangerous and several of us might not make it back alive. Our craft didn't go all the way to the shore, so we had to wade through the water to get to the sand. I was concerned for my cameras. I had three in total and I couldn't afford to get them wet.

Additional information

- Robert Capa took 106 photographs on Omaha beach but an accident during the developing process meant that all but 11 of them were destroyed. These remaining photographs, called 'The Magnificent Eleven', were published in LIFE magazine and made Capa famous. They are among the best-known images of the invasion.

- After the war, Capa founded a photographic agency that is still in business today. He continued to work as a photographer, taking pictures of wars and political events around the world and while working in Indochina (modern day Vietnam), Capa was killed by stepping on a land mine. He was only 40 years old.

- Modern armies often allow journalists to accompany them on missions. This practice is called 'embedding' and allows journalists to get really close to the action. However, the army decides which information, including words and pictures, are released.

- The soldier that Capa helped to shore is believed to be Private Huston Riley. Thanks to Capa's efforts, Riley survived the ordeal and was able to describe being saved by a man wearing a journalist's ID. He was surprised to see a photographer among the troops, but grateful for the help.

I remained on the beach for over an hour, taking as many photographs as I could while doing my best to avoid being hit or blown up. Bullets and bombs were exploding everywhere and there was barely anywhere to offer cover. It passed in a blur and I can't even remember how many photographs I took. Our camera technology means that we have to take a full series of images and develop them later. Sometimes, if there's a problem with the film, the images can be ruined. I only had one chance to capture the pictures of D-Day. I did my best.

I started taking photographs even before we reached the shore. I snapped the soldiers as they left the craft. As I stepped into the water I found myself quickly caught up in the action. I saw one man get into difficulty, his equipment weighing him down and preventing him from moving. The Germans trained their guns on him and I saw bullets ricochet off his helmet. Another shot hit and he fell down, injured. I worked with another soldier to help him to safety. I could only think of helping him, but I did remember what I was there for and managed to take some photos of him as he got onto the beach.

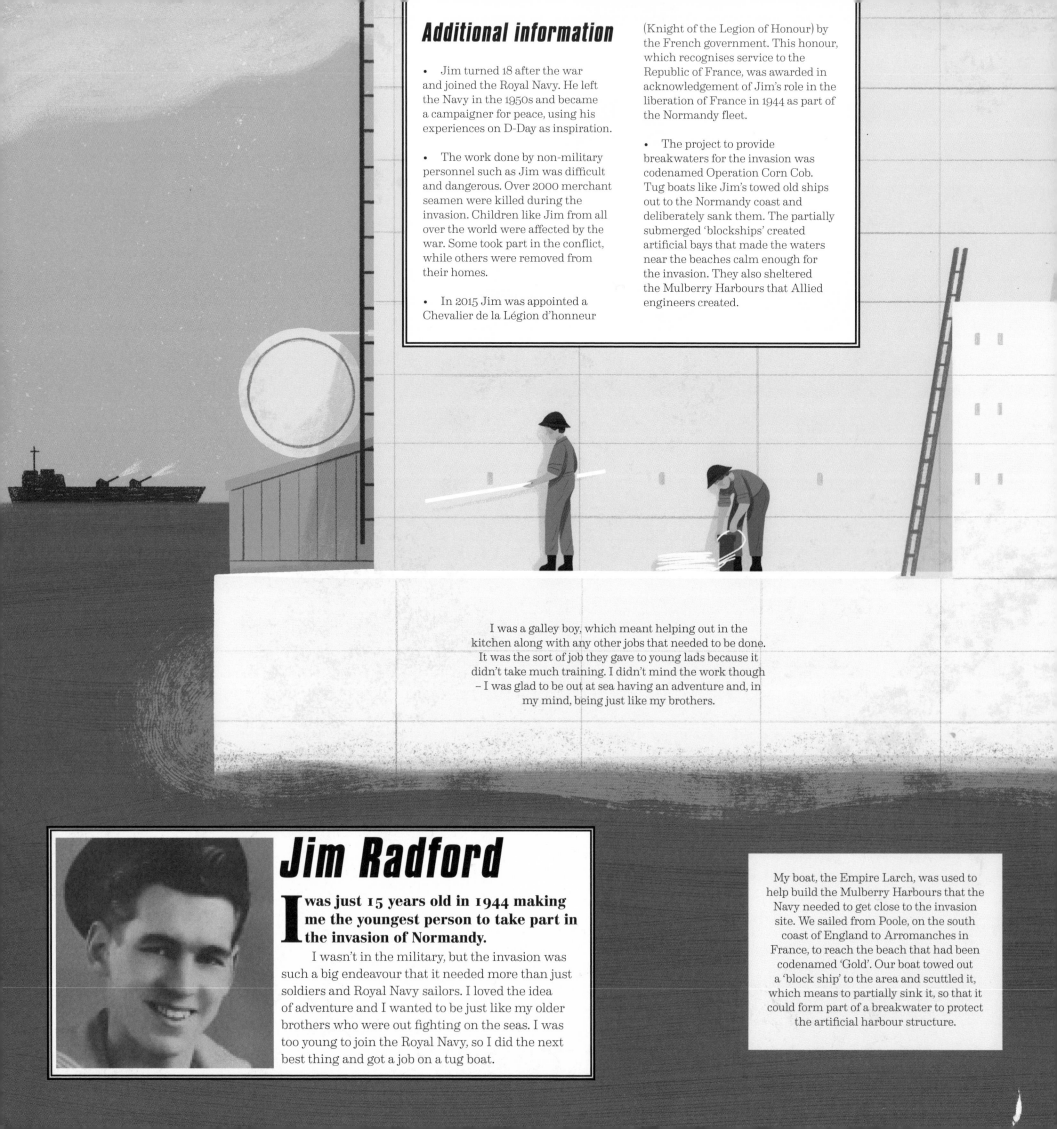

Additional information

- Jim turned 18 after the war and joined the Royal Navy. He left the Navy in the 1950s and became a campaigner for peace, using his experiences on D-Day as inspiration.

- The work done by non-military personnel such as Jim was difficult and dangerous. Over 2000 merchant seamen were killed during the invasion. Children like Jim from all over the world were affected by the war. Some took part in the conflict, while others were removed from their homes.

- In 2015 Jim was appointed a Chevalier de la Légion d'honneur (Knight of the Legion of Honour) by the French government. This honour, which recognises service to the Republic of France, was awarded in acknowledgement of Jim's role in the liberation of France in 1944 as part of the Normandy fleet.

- The project to provide breakwaters for the invasion was codenamed Operation Corn Cob. Tug boats like Jim's towed old ships out to the Normandy coast and deliberately sank them. The partially submerged 'blockships' created artificial bays that made the waters near the beaches calm enough for the invasion. They also sheltered the Mulberry Harbours that Allied engineers created.

I was a galley boy, which meant helping out in the kitchen along with any other jobs that needed to be done. It was the sort of job they gave to young lads because it didn't take much training. I didn't mind the work though – I was glad to be out at sea having an adventure and, in my mind, being just like my brothers.

Jim Radford

I was just 15 years old in 1944 making me the youngest person to take part in the invasion of Normandy.

I wasn't in the military, but the invasion was such a big endeavour that it needed more than just soldiers and Royal Navy sailors. I loved the idea of adventure and I wanted to be just like my older brothers who were out fighting on the seas. I was too young to join the Royal Navy, so I did the next best thing and got a job on a tug boat.

My boat, the Empire Larch, was used to help build the Mulberry Harbours that the Navy needed to get close to the invasion site. We sailed from Poole, on the south coast of England to Arromanches in France, to reach the beach that had been codenamed 'Gold'. Our boat towed out a 'block ship' to the area and scuttled it, which means to partially sink it, so that it could form part of a breakwater to protect the artificial harbour structure.

The death toll was staggeringly high. There were too many fallen soldiers to count. I remember thinking that it didn't seem real, but it was. It is such a painful memory and it has made me strongly opposed to war. I agree that defeating the Nazis was the right thing to do. They were guilty of horrible crimes and needed to be stopped, but the cost was so great that it is rarely justified.

Gold Beach was in the centre of the invasion line. The noise was incredible, every Navy ship was firing guns, sending huge clouds of smoke into the air. There was fire too – I could see smaller craft burning as they got closer to the shore. The air was alive with bullets and shells and our boat, though technically a civilian craft, was as much a target as any of the others.

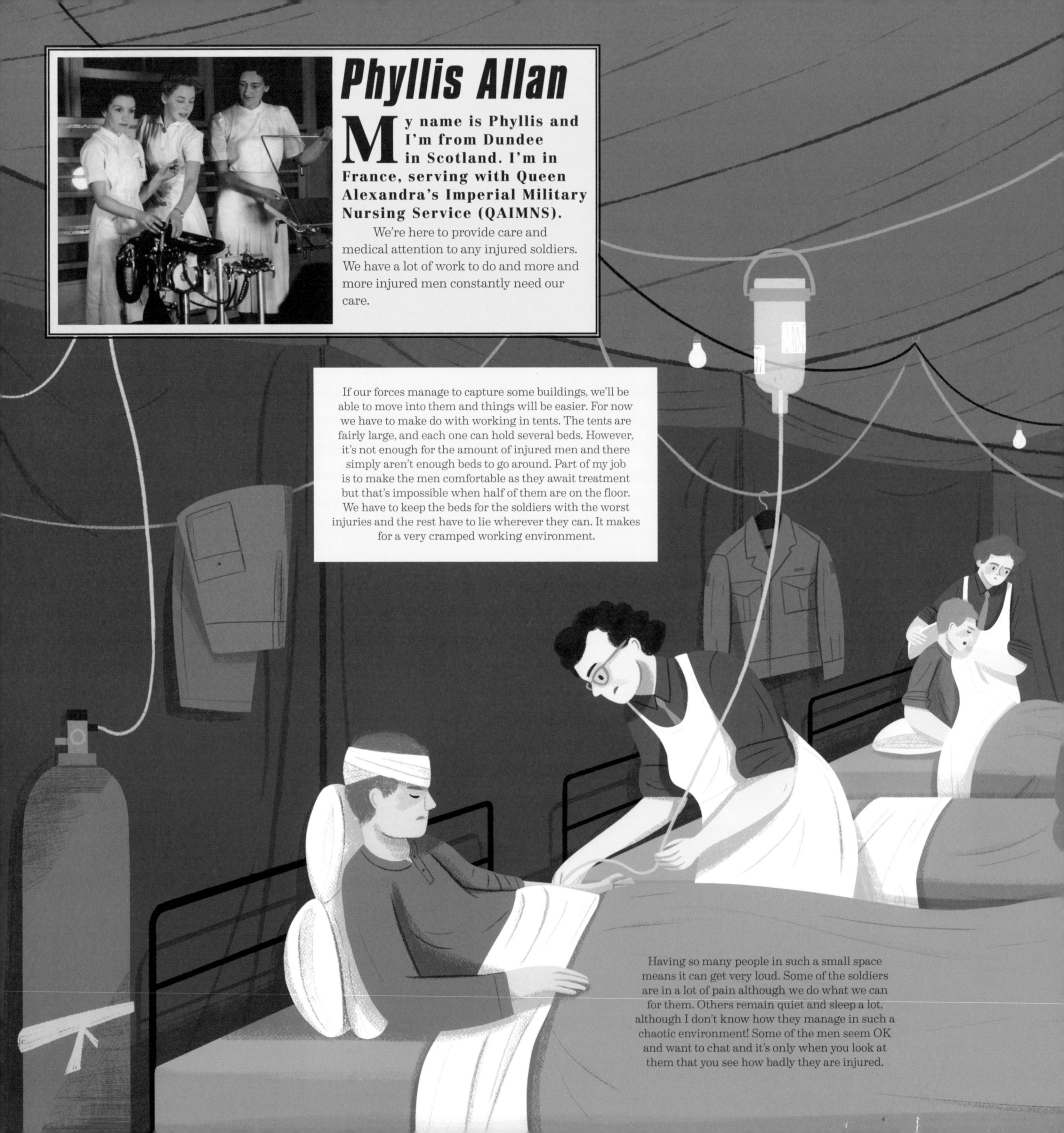

Phyllis Allan

My name is Phyllis and I'm from Dundee in Scotland. I'm in France, serving with Queen Alexandra's Imperial Military Nursing Service (QAIMNS).

We're here to provide care and medical attention to any injured soldiers. We have a lot of work to do and more and more injured men constantly need our care.

If our forces manage to capture some buildings, we'll be able to move into them and things will be easier. For now we have to make do with working in tents. The tents are fairly large, and each one can hold several beds. However, it's not enough for the amount of injured men and there simply aren't enough beds to go around. Part of my job is to make the men comfortable as they await treatment but that's impossible when half of them are on the floor. We have to keep the beds for the soldiers with the worst injuries and the rest have to lie wherever they can. It makes for a very cramped working environment.

Having so many people in such a small space means it can get very loud. Some of the soldiers are in a lot of pain although we do what we can for them. Others remain quiet and sleep a lot, although I don't know how they manage in such a chaotic environment! Some of the men seem OK and want to chat and it's only when you look at them that you see how badly they are injured.

We get all sorts of wounds to deal with here. Some men have lost limbs, or been burned from explosions and fires, while others have been hurt by falling from, or underneath, vehicles. Most have been shot or received shrapnel wounds and there is always a lot of blood. If there's one thing worse than the noise, it's the smell. We use a lot of disinfectant to keep things clean but the smell of that just adds to the odour. It's a relief every time I step outside the tent into the air.

I'm glad that I can use my skills to help people in desperate need of care and comfort and that I'm able to do my bit for this mission. It's so important but I don't think of myself as a hero. It's just a job, really.

Additional information

- Phyllis carried on working after D-Day, providing nursing support to the Allied forces as they pressed closer to Germany. She was shocked by the devastation in the French and Belgian towns that she passed through.

- Nursing staff like Phyllis wore simple uniforms that were designed to be practical and easy to keep clean. The photo on the opposite page shows some of the brave women who played their part in helping the injured.

- While training with the QAIMNS Phyllis met a soldier named Freddie Heninger. The pair soon married and, once the war was over, settled down to a peaceful life in the Scottish borders.

- With such intense fighting in Normandy, even the nursing staff had to be trained in combat skills. Nurses were taught how to climb and descend ropes, crawl under barbed wire and even self-defence techniques.

Brigitte de Kergorlay

My name is Brigitte de Kergorlay and I've just turned 24 years old. When I was 19 my life was turned upside down because the Germans invaded France and took over my home, Château de Canisy, where my family has lived for hundreds of years.

Uniformed soldiers stomped about the usually very peaceful surroundings and my father was so angry that he refused to speak to them. The role of communicator fell to me but luckily, I can speak German – although a part of me never wants to speak it again after this experience. The Germans turned our beloved home into a military headquarters, filling it with soldiers and official-looking men, while we were forced to occupy the smaller rooms and try our best to keep out of the way.

Things went on like that for four long years but earlier this summer things began to change… We woke to find countless planes filling the air and German soldiers rushing around frantically, shouting and giving orders. We had been hoping that the British and Americans would come and push the Germans out of France and it looked as if it was finally happening.

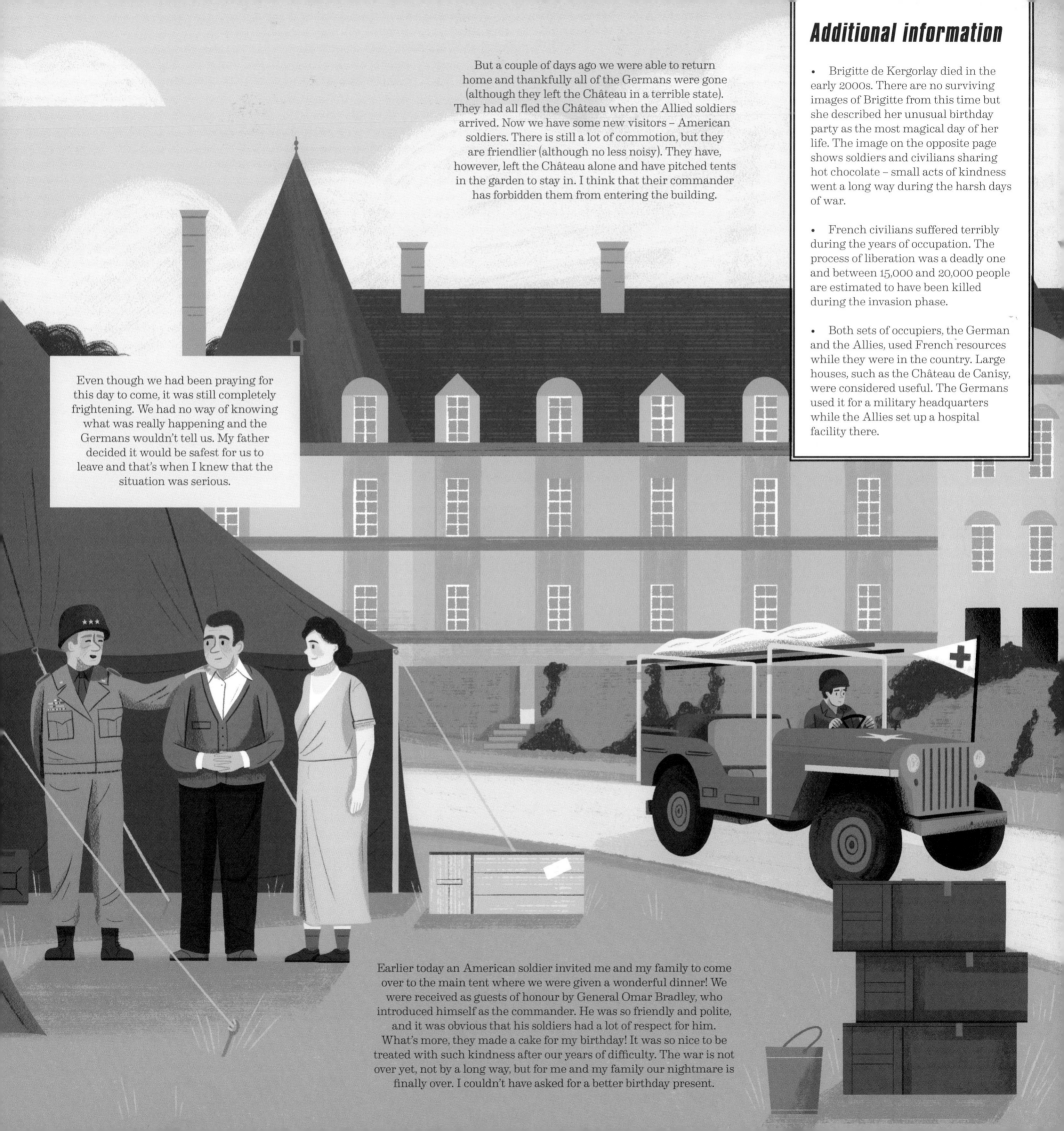

But a couple of days ago we were able to return home and thankfully all of the Germans were gone (although they left the Château in a terrible state). They had all fled the Château when the Allied soldiers arrived. Now we have some new visitors – American soldiers. There is still a lot of commotion, but they are friendlier (although no less noisy). They have, however, left the Château alone and have pitched tents in the garden to stay in. I think that their commander has forbidden them from entering the building.

Even though we had been praying for this day to come, it was still completely frightening. We had no way of knowing what was really happening and the Germans wouldn't tell us. My father decided it would be safest for us to leave and that's when I knew that the situation was serious.

Earlier today an American soldier invited me and my family to come over to the main tent where we were given a wonderful dinner! We were received as guests of honour by General Omar Bradley, who introduced himself as the commander. He was so friendly and polite, and it was obvious that his soldiers had a lot of respect for him. What's more, they made a cake for my birthday! It was so nice to be treated with such kindness after our years of difficulty. The war is not over yet, not by a long way, but for me and my family our nightmare is finally over. I couldn't have asked for a better birthday present.

Additional information

• Brigitte de Kergorlay died in the early 2000s. There are no surviving images of Brigitte from this time but she described her unusual birthday party as the most magical day of her life. The image on the opposite page shows soldiers and civilians sharing hot chocolate – small acts of kindness went a long way during the harsh days of war.

• French civilians suffered terribly during the years of occupation. The process of liberation was a deadly one and between 15,000 and 20,000 people are estimated to have been killed during the invasion phase.

• Both sets of occupiers, the German and the Allies, used French resources while they were in the country. Large houses, such as the Château de Canisy, were considered useful. The Germans used it for a military headquarters while the Allies set up a hospital facility there.

Ernie Pyle

I'm Ernie Pyle, a journalist with the American press. I've written a lot of articles about this war and have got to know many of the soldiers fighting it.

Living and working alongside them gives me a good insight into how they face the challenges of combat.

I always try to find the point of view of the ordinary solider and present that to my readers. Many of the people reading my work have loved ones fighting overseas and want to know what life is like for them.

It's important for me to show that, although the landings themselves were difficult, dangerous and costly, they were only the beginning of the effort. The task now is to press on and take the fight into Germany itself. The prospect is just as tough as the landings. There's no telling how long it will take, or what our forces will have to do to achieve their objective.

There are signs of death and destruction everywhere. On the day of the invasion the beaches were full of wrecked vehicles, discarded weapons, burning debris and the wreckage of crashed planes. It was like a terrible wasteland and it's hard to imagine people living here ever again. Not even the sea could escape the sense of ruin. Abandoned boat rafts and other items floated sulkily and the water was a disgusting colour – a mixture of blood, oil and filth.

The soldiers move along in oddly-spaced lines so that the enemy can't work out where to aim. They crouch and move forward like sneaking animals. They are not fearless warriors or superhuman fighters. They are ordinary young men, who, were it not for this war, would be living quiet lives at home. I suppose the same could be said for the enemy soldiers too.

Moving through French towns is dangerous because there are lots of places for the enemy to hide. As if from nowhere and without any warning bullets can start whizzing through the air. Sometimes you see a man drop down dead in front of you and you don't realise he's been shot until it has happened. It's terrifying. We all do our best to dive for cover, behind walls, in ditches, wherever we can. It seems impossible that we'll be able to keep doing this all the way through France, but we have to.

Additional information

• Ernie Pyle continued to report from France for a couple of months after D-Day and later moved on to report from the Pacific Ocean, where US-led troops were fighting the Japanese. He was killed by a gunshot on the island of Okinawa, which is part of Japan.

• War correspondents play an important role in keeping people informed about events in wartime. Readers rely on them to report accurately on events. They also befriend soldiers and tell their personal stories in their writings.

• The fighting in Western Europe continued for a further 11 months after the D-Day landings. The European war ended when troops from the Soviet Union entered the German capital, Berlin from the east. They were soon joined by Allied troops from the west, many of whom had landed in Normandy on D-Day. The event was celebrated as 'Victory in Europe', or 'VE Day'.

• Fighting continued in the Pacific until August, when Japan, which had been an ally of Germany, finally surrendered. By then, the United States had dropped two incredibly powerful bombs, known as 'atomic bombs', on the Japanese cities of Hiroshima and Nagasaki. The power of these weapons means that any future war on the scale of World War II would be very dangerous indeed. Since the end of the war, countries have tried very hard to prevent such a colossal war from happening again.

GLOSSARY

Allied Forces
The nations that formally united to fight against the Axis in World War II, including the UK, France, the Soviet Union and the USA.

Artillery
Large weapons used in warfare on land.

Atomic weapons
Weapons whose violent explosive power is because of the sudden release of energy resulting from the splitting of nuclei of a heavy chemical element (such as plutonium or uranium) by neutrons in a rapid chain reaction.

Axis Powers
The countries aligned against the Allied Forces in World War II, including Germany, Italy and Japan.

Civilian
Someone who is not in the armed services or the police force.

Codebreaker
Someone who solves codes.

Colossal
Something that is extremely large or great.

Comrade
Someone who is a fellow member of the an organisation – in war it would be a fellow soldier or member of the armed forces.

Conflict
A serious disagreement or argument.

Continent
One of the earth's seven major areas of land (Africa, Antarctica, Asia, Australia, Europe, North America and South America).

Convoy
A group of ships or vehicles travelling together.

Countermeasures
Action taken to work against a danger or threat.

Coward
Someone who doesn't have the courage to do something dangerous.

Dominate
To have power over something.

Dunes
A mound of sand formed by the wind, usually on the coast next to the sea.

Emplacements
A structure on or in which something is firmly placed.

Engineer
Someone whose job it is to design, build, or maintain engines, machines, or structures.

Harbour
A place on the coast where ships can shelter, especially one protected from rough water by piers, jetties, and other artificial structures.

Headquarters
Somewhere occupied by a military commander and their staff.

Humiliated
To feel ashamed and foolish.

Invasion
The act of invading a country or region with armed forces.

Liberation
To set someone free from imprisonment, slavery, or oppression.

Medic
Someone who practices medicine.

Meteorology
The area of science that studies the atmosphere and how we can forecast the weather.

Mine
A type of bomb placed on or just below the surface of the ground or in the water, which detonates on contact with something.

Occupation
A job.

Paratroops
Troops trained and equipped to be dropped by parachute from aircraft.

Patrol
To keep watch over an area, especially by guards or police walking or driving around at regular intervals.

Peninsula
A piece of land almost surrounded by water or sticking out into a body of water.

Permission
To officially allow someone to do a particular thing.

Photojournalist
A journalist who tells stories and gives news through photographs.

Radar
A system for detecting the presence, direction, distance, and speed of aircraft, ships, and other objects, by sending out pulses of radio waves which are reflected off the object.

Reconnaissance
Military observation of an area to locate an enemy.

Satellites
Something that is placed in orbit around the Earth or another planet to collect information or for communication.

Segregation
To separate people from others because of their race or religious beliefs.

Shell
An explosive artillery projectile or bomb.

Shrapnel
Pieces of a bomb, shell, or other object thrown out by an explosion.

Spy
Someone employed by a government or other organization to secretly get information on an enemy or competitor.

Squadron
A unit in an air force made up of two or more flights of aircraft and the people required to fly them.

Terrain
An area of land.

Territory
An area of land that belongs to a ruler or state.

Treacherous
Something that is dangerously unstable and unpredictable.

Troops
Soldiers or armed forces.

Tug boat
A small, powerful boat that is used to tow larger boats and ships.

Unit
A smaller section of a larger military grouping.

Volunteer
Someone who freely offers to take part in a task.

Warfare
Conflict between opposing sides.

Wasteland
An unused area of land that has become overgrown.

Wound
An injury caused by a cut or other impact, usually one where the skin is cut or broken.

Publisher's note:

These stories have been inspiried by real-life people and events.

Photographic acknowledgements:

Every effort has been made to find the copyright holder for each image. The publishers are happy to correct any errors on reprint.

All photos taken from Wikimedia Commons unless otherwise specified:

P8 Bundesarchiv, Bild 101I-217-0465-32A / Klintzsch / CC-BY-SA 3.0/ Wikimedia Commons, P16 BlackPast.org, P20 Bundesarchiv, Bild 146-1985-013-07 / CC-BY-SA 3.0/ Wikimedia Commons, P26 Keystone / Stringer/ Getty Images, P30 Bundesarchiv, Bild 183-L08129 / CC-BY-SA 3.0/ Wikimedia Commons, P34 Jim Radford, P38 Time Life Pictures / Contributor/ Getty Images.

Brimming with creative inspiration, how-to projects, and useful information to enrich your everyday life, Quarto Knows is a favourite destination for those pursuing their interests and passions. Visit our site and dig deeper with our books into your area of interest: Quarto Creates, Quarto Cooks, Quarto Homes, Quarto Lives, Quarto Drives, Quarto Explores, Quarto Gifts, or Quarto Kids.

D-Day © 2019 Quarto Publishing plc.
Text © 2019 Michael Noble. Illustrations © 2019 Alexander Mostov.

First Published in 2019 by Wide Eyed Editions, an imprint of The Quarto Group.
The Old Brewery, 6 Blundell Street, London N7 9BH, United Kingdom
T (0)20 7700 6700 F (0)20 7700 8066 **www.QuartoKnows.com**

The right of Alexander Mostov to be identified as the illustrator and Michael Noble to be identified as the author of this work has been asserted by them in accordance with the Copyright, Designs and Patents Act, 1988 (United Kingdom).

A catalogue record for this book is available from the British Library.

ISBN 978-1-78603-626-1

The illustrations were created digitally
Set in Aachen, Agenda, Centennial, Compacta, Eames Century Modern

Published by Rachel Williams
Designed by Nicola Price
Edited by Claire Grace
Production by Nicolas Zeifman

Manufactured in Grude, Bosnia GP022019

9 8 7 6 5 4 3 2 1